CREATING CREATURE CRAFTS

WILD ANIMAL CRAFTS

ANNALEES LIM

WINDMILL
BOOKS
New York

CONTENTS

Welcome to the world of wild animals! ... 3

Floating hippo 4

Bug-eyed frog 6

Balsa beaver 8

Croc card 10

Giraffe puppet 12

Climbing koala 14

Pom-pom panda 16

Pretty parrot 18

Armored armadillo 20

Feathery ostrich 22

Glossary and Index 24

Welcome to the world of wild animals!

Which animals have you seen in the wild before? Would you like to make some of your own and find out loads of fun facts about them along the way? Then this book is for you!

Follow the easy step-by-step instructions to start creating your own wild animal collection. When you have finished making an animal, you can also think about how and where that animal might live.

A lot of the projects use paint and glue. Always cover surfaces with a piece of plastic or layers of old newspaper. Whenever you can, leave the project to dry before moving on to the next step. This keeps things from getting stuck to each other and paint from smudging.

A note about measurements
Measurements are given in U.S. form with metric in parentheses. The metric conversion is rounded to make it easier to measure.

So, do you have your craft tools ready to go? Then get set to make your crafty creatures and discover what makes each of them so special!

FLOATING HIPPO

Hippos live in hot areas. They spend a lot of time in water to keep cool. Once you have made your hippo, try floating it in water, too!

You will need:
Small water bottle
Dark blue, white, black and light blue foam
Craft glue
Scissors

Optional:
Masking tape

1

Screw the lid tightly onto the water bottle. Wrap the whole bottle in light blue foam and stick it in place with the craft glue. You might need to use some masking tape to hold the foam in place until it dries.

2

Cut out shapes from the light blue foam: a "B" shape for your hippo's nose, a quarter of a circle (with the tip trimmed off), 2 ears and a tail.

4

3

Stick the "B" shape onto the bottle lid. Bend the quarter circle around the neck of the bottle to make the hippo's face.

4

Stick the rest of the blue pieces onto the bottle using the craft glue. Leave to dry.

5

Make some eyes from the black and the white foam, and some inner ears and nostrils from the dark blue foam. Stick them in place with craft glue.

HIPPO FACT
Did you know that the hippo is one of the most dangerous animals in the world? It has huge teeth and powerful jaws.

BUG-EYED FROG

You will need:
large paper plate
small paper plate
3 paper bowls
Craft glue
Green paint
Paintbrush
2 Ping-Pong balls
Pink and red paper
Tape
Black marker pen
Scissors

Frogs have big, round eyes that help them to see in many directions at once. Use Ping-Pong balls to make your frog's eyes enormous!

1

Paint the paper plates and bowls green and leave them to dry. Draw some black dots onto 2 Ping-Pong balls to make eyes.

2

Cut an equally sized piece off the side of 2 bowls. Stick them together to make your frog's body.

3

Cut the large paper plate into quarters, then cut the rim off each piece. These will form your frog's legs. Cut the center pieces to make 4 feet.

4

Glue the feet to the legs, and glue all 4 legs to your frog's body. Cut out a circle from pink paper. Make sure it's the size of a bowl. Cut a bowl and the small plate in half. Glue half of each to the pink circle to form the frog's head.

5

Cut out a tongue shape from red paper and stick it to the mouth. Use tape to attach the eyes to the top of the head and then the head to the body.

FROG FACT
Young frogs are called tadpoles. They are black and have a long tail.

BALSA BEAVER

Beavers have long, sharp teeth that they use to cut through wood. They use the wood to build homes, called lodges.

1

Draw the shapes for your beaver's body parts onto scrap card stock. Cut out all the shapes.

2

Using the shapes as templates, draw your beaver's body parts onto the balsa wood. Cut them out with the scissors. You might need an adult to help you with the cutting.

3

Use crayons to color in the body parts. You can use a felt-tipped pen to add a criss-cross pattern to the tail.

4

Glue all the body parts together to make your beaver. Glue on some googly eyes.

5

Glue the twigs to the back of your beaver to help him stand up. You can even place one twig in his paws!

BEAVER FACT
Beavers build huge dams made of twigs, mud and branches. Some are up to 13 feet (4 m) high!

CROC CARD

You will need:
- 2 pieces of green card stock, 8½ by 11 (21.5 x 28cm)
- Blue paper, 8½ by 11 (21.5 x 28cm)
- White paper
- Scissors
- Glue stick
- Black marker
- Ruler

Crocodiles have up to 80 teeth! You don't have to make all 80 for this crafty croc, but make sure they are all sharp and white.

1

Fold one piece of green card stock in half, lengthwise, and cut lots of slits along the fold. Start with two that are 1 inch (2.5 cm) apart. Make sure the slits in the middle are longer than those at the ends.

2

Open the piece of card stock and pop out the slitted sections. These will form your crocodile.

3

Cut a triangle shape out of the longest section to make the mouth. Using the other piece of green card stock, cut out a "B" shape that is as wide as your croc's head.

4

Stick the "B" shape to the croc's head. Cut out two rows of sharp teeth from white paper. Stick them to the inside of the mouth. Cut out eyes, feet, nostrils and a tail.

5

Stick all the body parts on except for the feet. Cut a shape out of blue paper to fit around your croc. Glue it to the card stock. Add the croc's feet and draw plants around it.

CROCODILE FACT
Did you know that crocodiles hold their mouths open in hot weather to help them cool down?

GIRAFFE PUPPET

You will need:
5 toilet paper rolls
Yellow and brown paper
Googly eyes
Glue stick
String
Stapler
Long wooden dowel, 12 inches (30cm) long
Scissors
Ruler
Adhesive tape

The pattern on each giraffe is unique – no two giraffes look the same. Why not create a special pattern for your giraffe?

1

Cut 3 toilet roll tubes in half and keep the other 2 whole. Cover all tubes in yellow paper. Decorate all but one short tube with patches of brown paper, stuck down with the glue stick.

2

Tie 4 pieces of string along the wooden dowel. The pieces should each be 12 inches (30cm) long. Feed the first string through the short yellow tube and staple in place.

3

Thread 2 long tubes onto the same string and staple them, too. Tie the ends of the first and the last string on the dowel together.

4

Thread 2 short tubes onto the ends of both middle strings to make the legs. Staple them in place. Use sticky tape to fix the strings to the body of your giraffe.

5

Cut into the head to make a mouth and cut two ears and a tail out of yellow paper. Use strips of brown paper to make the mane, the tail end and the hooves. Glue on the eyes.

GIRAFFE FACT

Giraffes are the tallest animals in the world. They are 3 times as tall as an adult human!

CLiMBiNG KOALA

Koalas live in eucalyptus trees in Australia. Craft your koala so that it can hang from plants in your home!

1

Draw a koala shape onto gray card stock, making sure that it is wider than the length of a clothespin. Cut it out and then draw around it to make a second koala shape.

2

Stick both koala shapes onto the dark gray felt and cut them out.

14

3

Cut out the shape of the koala's face from light gray felt. Stick it onto one of the koala shapes.

4

Cut out 2 ear tufts from white felt and eyes, a nose and a mouth from black felt. Stick them all on the koala's face.

5

Sandwich the clothespins in between both koala shapes. Fix the clothespins in place with fabric glue.

KOALA FACT
Did you know that koalas aren't bears? They are related to wombats and kangaroos.

POM-POM PANDA

You will need:
Small and large pom-poms in black and white
Fabric glue
Googly eyes
Green pipe cleaners
Florist foam
Black felt
Scissors

There are fewer than 2,000 pandas left in the wild. Make your own cuddly panda and keep it in a bamboo forest.

1

Glue 2 white pom-poms to each other. Then glue a small white pom-pom to one of the larger ones.

2

Glue 6 small black pom-poms onto the white body to make the ears, arms and legs of your panda.

3

Cut shapes out of the black felt for the eyes and nose. Glue them to the head and then glue on googly eyes.

4

Cut 5 pipe cleaners in half. Cut 5 others into 10 pieces each. Wrap the small pieces around the longer ones to make bamboo shoots.

5

Press all but one of the bamboo plants into the florist foam. Set the panda in the scene. Place the last bamboo plant in your panda's paws.

PANDA FACT
In the wild, pandas only eat bamboo shoots.

17

PRETTY PARROT

These brightly colored birds live in warm parts of the world. Follow the steps to make a scarlet macaw with colorful wings!

1

Bend one end of 2 pipe cleaners. Twist a shorter length of pipe cleaner to each of them to form claws.

2

Roll a large piece of red card stock around a paper towel roll. Stick it in place with glue.

3

Cut wing shapes in different sizes from blue, green, yellow and red card stock. Cut slits into the edges. Cut 3 tail feather shapes from red card stock.

4

Cut a shape for the face from red card stock. Use white paper to make the beak and two circles to hold the eyes. Cut out a black shape that looks like an "8."

5

Glue all the shapes together, and stick on googly eyes. Glue the pipe cleaners to the inside of your parrot's body. You can make a branch for it to sit on by rolling up some brown card stock.

PARROT FACT
Macaws have very powerful beaks that can crack nut shells!

ARMORED ARMADILLO

The armadillo is the only animal to have plates of "armor" on its body! Some can even roll up into a ball to protect hemselves.

You will need:
Brown foam
Black marker
Paper fasteners
Ruler
Scissors
Googly eyes
Craft glue

Optional:
Masking tape

1

Cut 5 brown strips of foam that measure 2¾ by 8 inches (7 x 20cm).

2

Arrange all the strips into a fan shape. Join them together using a paper fastener.

3

Bend all the strips and join them together on the other side using another paper fastener. Trim the corners of the strips.

4

Cut out 4 feet, 2 ears, a tail and a semicircle to form your armadillo's head.

5

Fold the semicircle to form a cone shape. Glue all the shapes onto your armadillo and add googly eyes. You may need to use masking tape to hold everything in place until the glue has dried.

ARMADILLO FACT
The word "armadillo" is Spanish for "little armored one"!

FEATHERY OSTRICH

Ostriches are the largest birds in the world! They live in small groups, called herds. Why not make your own crafty ostrich herd?

1

Stack 3 wooden spoons, with the head of the middle one higher than the others. wrap black electrical tape around the center of the stack, and white electrical tape around the rest of the spoons.

2

Form 2 feet out of modeling clay, making sure they are quite thick.

3

Press the two handles into the modeling clay feet to make your ostrich stand up.

4

Stick lots of black feathers onto the body to make your ostrich's wings.

5

Cut and fold a beak from pink paper. Stick it onto the face using the fabric glue. Stick on googly eyes.

OSTRICH FACT

An ostrich's legs are very powerful. When they run, their strides can be 16 feet (5m) long!

GLOSSARY

bamboo shoot	the young part of a bamboo plant that has just sprouted
dam	a mound of twigs, mud and leaves that beavers build across rivers
puppet	a kind of doll that has strings attached to it; you can move the doll by pulling the strings
unique	when something is one of a kind, not like anything else

INDEX

armadillo 20, 21

bamboo 16, 17
beak 19, 23
bear 15
beaver 8, 9

crocodile 10, 11

frog 6, 7

giraffe 12, 13

hippo 4, 5
hooves 13

jaws 5

koala 14, 15

lodge 8

ostrich 20, 21

panda 16, 17
parrot 18, 19
puppet 12, 13

tadpole 7
teeth 5, 8, 10, 11

Published in 2016 by Windmill Books,
an Imprint of Rosen Publishing
29 East 21st Street, New York, NY 10010

Copyright © 2016 Wayland/Windmill

Series editor: Julia Adams
Craft photography: Simon Pask, N1 Studios
Additional images: Shutterstock

Cataloging-in-Publication Data
Lim, Annalees.
Wild animal crafts / by Annalees Lim.
p. cm. — (Creating creature crafts)
Includes index.
ISBN 978-1-5081-9117-9 (pbk.)
ISBN 978-1-5081-9118-6 (6-pack)
ISBN 978-1-5081-9119-3 (library binding)
1. Handicraft – Juvenile literature. 2. Animals in art –
Juvenile literature. 3. Wildlife art – Juvenile literature.
I. Lim, Annalees. II. Title.
TT174.3 L56 2016
743.6—d23

Manufactured in the United States of America

CPSIA Compliance Information Batch #BW16PK For Further Information
contact Rosen Publishing New York, New York at 1-800-237-9932